Meeting special needs

A practical guide to support children with Dyslexia

by Collette Drifte

*In memory of Kiernan and Spencer Frampton,
both very special people with
their own special needs.*

*In this book the use of he, him or his is gender neutral and is
intended to include both sexes.*

Published by Step Forward Publishing Limited
St Jude's Church, Dulwich Road, Herne Hill, London, SE24 0PB Tel. 020 7738 5454
© Step Forward Publishing Limited 2007 www.practicalpreschool.com

Meeting special needs. A practical guide to support children with Dyslexia ISBN: 978-1-904-575-16-0

Contents

Pages to copy and use:

Introduction

If you are looking at this book, it is a safe bet that you have an interest in dyslexia. Perhaps in a professional capacity, you are working with a child who seems to have difficulties with his literacy skills, and you wonder whether dyslexia has something to do with it.

Whatever your reason for picking up this book, I hope you will find answers to some of your questions about dyslexia, and ideas for things you can actually do to support the child in managing his difficulty. The book is a starting point and it gives you background information and practical suggestions for action you can take.

Remember you are not on your own. Your setting should have an inclusive special educational needs (SEN) policy in place, and a designated Special Educational Needs Coordinator (SENCO) who should work closely with you to help the child achieve his potential. While it is not the job of the SENCO to work on a one-to-one basis with the child (unless, of course, he also happens to be the child's key practitioner), he is there to offer you support and advice. Even if he does not know the answers to your questions, he will know where to go and whom to ask.

There are also organisations such as Dyslexia Action

(formerly known as the Dyslexia Institute), the British Dyslexia Association and parents' support groups that will help you. You will find contact details of these and other supporting organisations at the end of the book. Take the opportunity to get in touch and listen to their advice and suggestions. They have excellent websites, with loads of help and guidance for you as the child's practitioner.

Scattered through the book are case studies which serve as examples to illustrate a point being made. They all feature real children whose names have been changed. You will also come across a Pause for Thought section every so often, where an issue will be introduced that gives you an opportunity to ponder practice a little more deeply, and which you can possibly discuss and share with your colleagues.

Before we move on to the main body of the book, allow me to say a few words about terminology. I still hear people referring to a dyslexic child, or, less positive, a dyslexic. It behoves us as professionals to relentlessly pursue and model the correct approach, ie. that the child is a child first and foremost who happens to have a condition or disability known as dyslexia. So you will find this book refers to a child with dyslexia or a child with dyslexic traits.

What exactly is dyslexia?

Most people know that dyslexia has something to do with reading difficulties, if only through publicity about celebrities who have the condition. But If you asked somebody what dyslexia is, he might find it hard to give a correct answer. It can also be confusing because dyslexia is sometimes given other names such as Specific Reading Difficulties or Specific Learning Difficulties.

Dyslexia was recognised over a century ago, but it is only since the 1970s that interest in it began to grow and research into it increased. In this section we will be looking at some of the facts and myths about dyslexia.

Dyslexia is a neurological condition, so a child is born with it, but it is only when he starts to use language and to learn to read and write that his problems show. It is a condition that affects a person's ability to read, write and spell. Sometimes a child's ability to do maths is also affected. (The condition that affects mathematical ability is called dyscalculia.) The reading and writing difficulties of a person with dyslexia are not caused by:

- emotional problems;
- other learning difficulties;
- vision or hearing impairments;
- poor teaching;
- laziness;
- lack of motivation.

The range of difficulty can be from a very slight problem to severe difficulties with learning various skills connected with reading, writing and spelling. The majority of children with dyslexia have difficulties with language, memory skills, organisation and sequencing.

Children who have dyslexia usually have problems when analysing the sounds of spoken words. You can appreciate immediately, therefore, the obstacles that he will encounter when he starts to tackle the phonics he is required to learn as part of his literacy skills curriculum.

He may find it very difficult to learn how to transpose spoken sounds into written letters. Consequently, his ability to spell and to decode, or 'sound out', words can be severely affected. All is not lost, however, as many children with dyslexia can in fact develop the decoding skills needed for phonics work, but they usually need much more teaching than a child without dyslexia, and some children will never learn how to decode automatically.

Dyslexia cannot be cured, as it is a lifelong difficulty, but the child can be helped with specialist teaching, and a willingness on his part to learn. It is crucial to identify dyslexia and start to help the child as early as possible.

How many children have dyslexia?

Figures vary, but it is thought that about 4% of the total population in the United Kingdom is severely affected by dyslexia (ie. about 2.5 million people), and about 10% of the population shows some sign of It (about 6 million people). 5% of the country's children have it, but of that 5% only 11% receive specialised help;

- it is thought that about 375,000 children in the UK have dyslexia;

- research shows that boys and girls are not equally affected, since there appear to be more boys who

have the condition. It is thought that the ratio is about 4:1, although no definite figures are available;

- any child can have dyslexia, regardless of his intelligence;

- children from any race or cultural group can have dyslexia;

- something like 60% of people with dyslexia find it hard to sort out the sounds within words – that is, they have phonological difficulties.

What causes dyslexia?

Dyslexia is a neurological condition that affects the way the child's brain works – research shows that the brain of a person with dyslexia is different from that of somebody not affected. Brain-scan research suggests that this difference is shown by the language-processing areas in the left hemisphere of the brain not performing as efficiently as they should. This, in turn, appears to be linked to genetic differences.

These differences, however, have nothing to do with intelligence, and there is evidence that many people with dyslexia have strengths and abilities in tasks that involve creative and visually-based thinking.

Dyslexia tends to run in families, so you can have several members of the same family experiencing similar difficulties. Researchers in the field now know that there are several genes that contribute to the risk of a child having dyslexia. Some researchers think that environmental factors are also linked to the occurrence of dyslexia. While dyslexia is an inherited neurological condition, it can be accompanied by problems with vision and hearing, or intellectual development. There are many ways of tackling these problems, in an attempt to help children who are also trying to manage their dyslexia.

How does specialist teaching work?

Before a child is given specialist teaching he must be assessed to make sure that his problems really are caused by dyslexia. A correct identification is crucial for matching up the correct type of teaching.

The assessment is usually carried out either by an educational psychologist or by a teacher who has a specialist qualification in dyslexia, but this will depend on what services and facilities are offered by your local authority (LA).

Check with your SENCO if you are unsure of the procedure. In an early years setting, it is unlikely that you will notice any glaringly obvious difficulties, as the child will not yet be doing formal literacy skills development. But it is still good practice to know what to do, should the need arise.

An assessment is usually made up of:

- a report or questionnaire completed by you, as the child's practitioner;
- a family questionnaire completed by the child's carers;
- a series of tests and tasks done by the child during a session with the educational psychologist or specialist teacher – these can take up to two hours to complete;
- a follow-up report giving the results and findings of the tests, and the recommendations about what to do next.

Once the child's dyslexia has been identified, he will need specialist teaching.

This should be:

- *structured,* so that reading and spelling make sense to the child. Specific letters and groups of letters are introduced, the child is shown ways of tackling longer or difficult words and spelling rules and the work is kept to whatever has been learnt in the lesson. This approach helps the child to build up his confidence, especially in having a go at more tricky words;
- *cumulative,* so that the child's reading and spelling skills are gradually built up. Each lesson leads on from the last one, so the child is well prepared to tackle the next stage. This gives the child confidence that he will not be expected to do work he has not prepared for;
- *multi-sensory,* so that sight, sound and touch are used as tools to teach the child. This gives him lots of ways to tackle hard or challenging words, and also helps him to develop his listening and speaking, looking and doing skills;
- *thorough,* so that the child gets plenty of practice and can over-learn a skill or technique. This helps the child to develop ways of using sounds, letters and spelling rules automatically;
- *active,* so that the child is really involved and therefore interested in learning. The activities and exercises are interesting and stimulating so that the child enjoys doing them and at the same time, has success. This helps him to continue making progress;
- *useful,* so that the child can see how the specialist teaching ties in with his everyday schoolwork. This helps the child to see the connection between his specialist lessons and the skills he is developing in his main lessons.

Find out whether the education department of your LA offers specialised teaching to children with dyslexia, as its specialist services are free of charge. If not, explore other ways in which the child's carer can access help. A fund exists which offers bursaries to people who cannot afford a specialist assessment and specialist lessons, although this is limited. If you think the child's carers would be interested in this, they can get information about it from Dyslexia Action, see useful contacts page at the end of the booklet.

Fears, wrong ideas and mistakes about dyslexia

Lots of so-called 'facts' have been quoted over the years about dyslexia. Many of them are simply untrue, but unfortunately they have become accepted as correct. Let's look at some of these and do a bit of myth exploding.

- children with dyslexia are lazy or stupid. This is completely untrue. It is possible (and has in fact happened) that children with dyslexia can be labelled as being lazy or stupid because of the difficulties they have with reading and writing. In fact, children with dyslexia can be highly intelligent, and very talented and skilled in other areas;

- dyslexia is catching. Dyslexia is a neurological condition and is not infectious or contagious. It can be passed on only genetically, within families;

- children with dyslexia are emotionally disturbed. It is true that some children with dyslexia have behaviour difficulties, but these are usually caused by the frustration the child feels when trying to manage the condition, or by his low self-esteem. Most behaviour and emotional difficulties are resolved when the child gets the right kind of teaching and he begins to overcome his problems;

- poor teaching causes dyslexia. Poor teaching can certainly help to make a difficult situation even worse, but it does not cause dyslexia. The problem is there from birth. But it is true to say that incorrect teaching or inappropriate teaching will not help the child;

- children with dyslexia have vision or hearing problems. Some children with dyslexia are found to have additional difficulties with their sight or hearing, but this is not always the case. It is important to have the child's vision and hearing checked by a professional to pick up any problems that do exist, and get him sorted out as quickly as possible.

You might look for information about dyslexia on the internet. Be careful to check on the accuracy of the information on the websites. Some of them give the impression that their organisation is the only place where the child can get specialist assessment and teaching. Find out what your LA can offer as well, and then the child's carers can make a fully-informed choice. Private assessments and the follow-up teaching can be very expensive, and you may be able to get good, specialist help for the child through your setting's contacts, or the LA.

How can dyslexia be recognised?

It is important to remember that only an educational psychologist or another specialist professional can identify whether the child you have concerns about actually has dyslexia.

This section describes some of the signs you can look out for to help you decide whether you ought to refer the child for further observation and identification of possible difficulties. By keeping careful records of your observations, you will have a description of the child and the way he presents himself in the setting that will help the outside agents in any assessment or testing that may be done.

You also need to bear in mind that no two children are the same. It does not follow that all children will experience all the problems, nor to the same degree of severity.

What signs do I need to look out for?

Dyslexia is not usually spotted until the child is at school and formally starts to learn to read and write. It is then that the problems begin to show themselves.

But there are still things to watch for if the child is below statutory school age. In this section, we will look at the signs to spot at various ages. It is important, however, to bear in mind that these are only generalised signs, and you may find a child of a particular age showing signs usually exhibited by a child of a different age. As with all these things, there is no hard-and-fast rule.

Babyhood, infancy and pre-school

Here, you may have to ask the child's carers to help you. Ask them to tell you about their child as a baby, a toddler and an infant. Their descriptions may help you to decide what action (if any) to take next. Some of these questions may apply to the child in the setting, so compare notes with the carers and see whether the child is the same at home as with you.

Find out whether the child

- did not crawl but shuffled on his bottom or wriggled on his tummy, or even walked early, leaving out the crawling stage altogether;
- developed speech later or slower than the carer expected;
- found it hard to remember nursery rhymes, or rhyming words such as cot, hot and pot (does that still happen in the setting?);
- found it hard to clap a simple rhythm (is he still like that?);
- could not remember the names of everyday things such as car or coat, (is that still the case?);
- jumbled up phrases regularly, such as cobblers' club instead of toddlers' club (how about now?);
- substitutes similar words, such as toothbrush for toothpaste;
- likes to be read to and enjoys stories etc., but is not interested in letters and words;
- often trips up, bumps into things or falls over;
- cannot kick, catch or throw a ball properly, cannot hop or skip;
- finds it hard to dress himself or put his shoes on properly;
- often seems to be ignoring adults who are looking after him; not listening or paying attention.

Age 5–11 years

Watch for whether the child

- has difficulty getting dressed, tying shoelaces, bows, etc.;
- is unusually clumsy;
- has poor concentration;

- does not have much confidence or has low self-esteem;
- finds it hard to talk to you in an organised way, or to hold a rapid conversation;
- finds it difficult to pronounce words;
- reverses words or substitutes them;
- cannot hear the difference between similar words, such as ten and tin;
- cannot carry out three instructions one after the other;
- finds it hard to understand time and tense;
- cannot remember his tables, spellings, the alphabet, etc.;
- mixes up right and left;
- has a poor sense of direction;
- finds it hard to recognise rhyming words;
- can tell you the answers to questions but cannot write them down;
- finds reading and spelling very hard;
- mixes up letters and figures, or puts them the wrong way around or upside down, such as d for b, q for p, 81 for 18, 6 for 9, was for saw, nut for fun, etc.;
- leaves letters out of words altogether;
- reads a word correctly then gets it wrong further down the page;
- spells the same words in several different ways, often not recognising the correct spelling;
- finds it hard to understand what he has just read;
- has difficulty with the order of the days of the week or the months of the year;
- needs to use his fingers to add and subtract;
- is bright and alert in areas not connected with reading and spelling.

Age 11– adult

Clearly this stage is well beyond the early years level, but it is still useful for you to have an idea of how a child with dyslexia may perform at a later stage of his development.

Check whether the child

- mixes up direction words such as backwards and forwards, in and out, up and down;
- still has difficulty with sequences such as the days of the week, months of the year, numbers, etc.;
- mixes up times, dates and places;
- continues to have problems with reading and spelling;
- finds it hard to remember what he has just read;
- has difficulty in concentrating when reading or writing;
- gets muddled when using long words;
- has to have telephone numbers and instructions repeated;
- has difficulty in taking notes accurately;
- finds it hard to plan and write essays or assignments;
- is bright and alert in areas not connected with reading and spelling;

- does not have much confidence or has low self-esteem.

Use the results of your observations during discussions with the carers; compare notes, experiences and anecdotes. Often a pattern or similar picture emerges, where the child is having the same difficulties both at home and in the setting.

It is particularly useful to watch how the child reacts when he is looking at books, and when he is doing his writing. The expression on his face can give away a great deal about what is going on in his head. For example, if he appears to be in pain or uncomfortable, ask him – children with dyslexia may get headaches when they are reading.

Track his eye movements when he is reading: do his eyes flit all over the page? A child with dyslexia may feel that the text moves about on the page, and he finds it difficult to focus on the words.

See what his reaction is when he has to do something involving a specific orientation. Does he appear confused? Does he watch the other children and then copy where they go, or what they do? Children with dyslexia often confuse left and right, and suffer torments when deciding which is required.

It is crucial to keep in mind that all children, including the one you may be concerned about, have some skills they can shine at. Take the trouble to see what the child's talents are, and help him to feel good about it.

Case study

Julian was nine years old and having great difficulty in school. He was a bright, alert and curious child, and yet was making very little progress with his literacy skills.

He had a formidable repertoire of avoidance strategies whenever he was asked to do something connected with reading or writing. He became the class clown, and eventually began to lag seriously behind his peers in achievement, as well as causing concern with his inappropriate behaviour.

His mother had his vision checked and everything was normal; his teacher, however, noticed that his head moved jerkily and erratically when he was reading. His spelling was bizarre and inconsistent. The school referred Julian to the LA learning support service, and he was assessed.

It was discovered that he had dyslexia and a programme of multi-sensory teaching was designed. Julian began to follow it, while also doing support activities at home with his mum. Within weeks, he was beginning to make progress, his behaviour settled, and he became a happier and more approachable child.

Why do I need to make the child feel good about his skills?

Children with dyslexia could develop other problems which can be much more damaging than the dyslexia itself. It is vital that they are prevented from developing any additional problems, particularly psychological or emotional ones.

Because they find it hard to succeed in the setting or in school, many children with dyslexia experience feelings of:

• frustration;
• sadness;
• anger;
• shame.

which in turn may lead to;

• anxiety;
• depression;
• low self-esteem;
• loneliness;
• behavioural problems;
• emotional difficulties;
• anti-social behaviour.

What are the signs and symptoms of these problems?

Here, in a bit more detail, are some of the problems that a child with dyslexia might develop.

• *Anxiety.* A child suffering from anxiety may act nervously and seem to be worried most of the time. He might dislike being separated from his parents or carers. He may get wound up if he has to speak out in the setting, at school or in front of other people. He could dislike being in crowds of people and get very upset in situations that are out of the ordinary;

• *Depression.* A child suffering from depression may seem irritable or sad most of the time. He might lose interest in activities that he used to enjoy. He can feel guilty for no reason and he may feel worthless. He may either lose his appetite or overeat. He can find it very hard to concentrate, and be unable to make decisions;

• *Low self-esteem.* A child can show his low self-esteem by;
  - giving up when a task gets too hard or challenging;
  - avoiding a task for fear of failing;
  - impulsively finishing a task any-old-how, just to get it over and done with;
  - finding it hard to accept correction;
  - over-reacting when he fails at a task;
  - seeming to feel safer if he 'takes control';
  - keeping quiet as if he is afraid to express an opinion;
  - constantly needing reassurance;

• *Loneliness.* A child with dyslexia can suffer from loneliness because he can be rejected by his group and may find it very hard to make and keep friends. This social rejection can lead to anxiety and depression, so adding to the child's difficulties;

• *Behavioural problems.* A child can develop behavioural problems because of low self-esteem. These can include being aggressive and bullying to ward off his feelings of vulnerability, or becoming the group clown to mask his lack of confidence.

If you recognise anything in this section that might apply to the child you're concerned about, mention it to his carers. They may well be noticing the same thing at home. If you refer the child to outside professionals, mention your observations to them too, as they will find the information useful in identifying the child's difficulties, and giving him support. Remember to ask the child's carers' permission before you speak about their child to anybody outside the setting.

How we feel about ourselves is known as self-esteem, and having high self-esteem is a crucial part of being well-balanced, happy and able to achieve. Think about the activities the child is good at, can do well and successfully, and that he enjoys. Take time to watch him when he is doing some of these things and tell him how good he is. He may need to have his confidence boosted, and you can make a start by pointing out that he is pretty good at that particular activity.

Why do some children develop these problems?

To be able to support the child, it will help if you understand some of the underlying reasons why these problems can develop as a result of his dyslexia.

- as we have seen, dyslexia is identified because the child has difficulty with his reading and writing. When you think about it, the child is spending most of his waking hours in an educational setting or school and, because of his dyslexia, he may experience failure over and over again. Our education system measures success by academic achievement, with SATs, targets, assessments and league tables all trying to show how well or otherwise a setting and its students are doing. This constant pressure to achieve adds to the problems of the child with dyslexia, so it is not surprising that some children develop psychological problems;
- the child is rarely, if ever, told anything good about himself; for example, that he has been trying really hard, that he is good at staying with a task until it is completed, or that he is brilliant at football. In other words, children with dyslexia may get very little positive feedback, but are constantly told to try harder, to stop being so lazy, to concentrate better and so on. In the end, the child gives up trying to achieve anything;
- children with dyslexia can be labelled by both the adults and the children around him. He can be called 'lazy', 'stupid', 'slow' or 'idle'. Negative labelling like this makes the child believe he has not anything to feel proud of and, as a result, he can develop a sense of being useless and worth nothing. He can even feel ashamed because he is not achieving in the setting or at school. All these negative feelings can lead to the child having low self-esteem;
- some children experience social difficulties because of their dyslexia. They may be rejected by the other children in their group who don't want to include them in games and activities. These social problems are interconnected with the psychological difficulties experienced by such children, and it can all result in more problems.

From all this, you can see how important it is to keep an eye on the child and make sure he is not under stress because of his dyslexia.

Pause for thought

Think of one child you have worked with in the past who puzzled you, perhaps because he seemed to be a contradiction on legs: he appeared to be intelligent, was able to perform well orally, but when it came to 'work', he seemed unable to achieve anything.

Did you share your thoughts with anybody in the setting? Did you speak to the child's carers about your feelings? How did you work with the child in the end? Looking back, do you feel your planning for the child was appropriate? Did it help the child to achieve and develop? If the answer is Yes, could or would you have done anything more or differently? If No, what would you change about the approach you took? Take a few minutes to write down your thoughts. When you have read all this book, come back to this question again, and have another ponder in the light of your new knowledge.

How can the setting support the child?

It goes without saying that you and the child's carers need to have a good and supportive relationship. By helping each other, you will all help the child.

It is very important that you understand how dyslexia affects the child you have concerns about, because you can then plan appropriate work and activities and treat the child with consideration and support.

Your everyday dealings with the child should be positive and encouraging, without criticism or judgement if some skills have not yet developed fully. The reading and writing problems that the child has because of his dyslexia need to be supported in the setting.

Under the current educational legislation, dyslexia is classed as special educational needs (SEN) and therefore you need to plan the child's curriculum according to the guidelines in the SEN Code of Practice. You can access and download the Code as a PDF file from the website of the Department for Children, Schools and Families (DCSF – formerly the Department for Education and Skills).

You will need to monitor the child closely, assess his performance and differentiate his work within the setting. You may have to refer him to an outside specialist and then work together as a team with the child, his carers and anybody else who may become involved. You will plan a programme of action specifically aimed at supporting the child, and developing the skills he already has, as a tool for developing the skills he needs. The Code of Practice clearly outlines each stage of the process, and of course your SENCO will be closely involved too.

Check with the child's carers whether there are things about the child that you may need to know. For example, find out whether

- the child's dyslexia is present alongside another condition, for example dyspraxia or learning difficulties;
- the child needs extra time to work out the words in a book;
- the child needs to sit directly in front of you;
- you should speak slowly;
- you need to give instructions one bit at a time;
- the child needs to have things repeated two or three times before he fully understands;

- the child finds it difficult to work in a particular way, such as in a group of other children, or on his own, either with an adult or another child;
- the child does not like to be touched.

It is important that the carers tell you of anything like this so that you can adapt the day's activities to include their child, as well as come to understand the way the child learns and performs.

Some practical suggestions

In our everyday living we are constantly bombarded with reading and writing, with no escape, and if we are to function (and indeed to survive) in society, we have to be able to make sense of all this literature.

We are exposed to the written word non-stop. Because of this, it is important for you to remember that the child with dyslexia is also bombarded, and as such will be under constant stress as he tries to make sense of it all.

Here are some ideas you can put into place to help him within the setting;

- let him use tape or compact disc recorders as much as possible when doing literacy-based work. This allows him to listen to something again and again, or to re-record his own work if he is not satisfied with the first draft;
- let him know that re-drafting is something you actively encourage. Nobody ever gets their writing correct the first time, and having another go at perfecting a piece of work is OK;
- allow the child to go over any worksheets or written information with an adult before the lesson or session starts. This allows

him to be ahead of the game and under less stress during the actual session. Neither will he be distracted from what you are saying in the session by trying to work out the hieroglyphics jumping about on the paper in front of him;

- if another adult is not available to help the child look at written information before a session, put as much of it onto disk as you can, and let the child spend time looking at it on the computer beforehand. There is screen reading software available to help him with this;
- try to utilise as much information and communication technology (ICT) as you can during literacy-based sessions. There is a plethora of programs, software and hardware available these days that can be put to good use to support the child. Log on to the Iansyst website, www.iansyst.co.uk and see what is on offer for people with dyslexia. Speak to your SENCO or your LA ICT specialist to see what is available through his contacts;

- when you have asked the child to do a piece of writing, let him know that, at this stage, the spellings do not matter; what you are interested initially in are his ideas. Sorting out the spellings can come later, during redraft or checking time. Spellings and grammar are the secretarial tasks that can be sorted out afterwards. You want him to enjoy writing, not be put off it for life because of an unnecessary obsession with instant correct spellings;
- if you use an interactive whiteboard in your sessions, remember to read aloud the written material that is displayed on it. This will help to take the pressure off the child, and enable him to concentrate on the content of the session, rather than figuring out the squiggles on the screen;
- try to print text on pastel-coloured paper. People with dyslexia often report a sensation of 'glare' from black-and-white text, but find that this is reduced if the written material is printed on soft background paper. Buff colour is often recommended.

How do I begin to work with the child and his carers?

It is important that you share as much information as you can about the child's difficulties. Ask the carers whether they have any records or files about the child, and whether you may read them.

The information in these can often give you an idea of how to work with the child. Conversely, let the carers know about the child's performance in the setting, so they can use the information to help the child at home. Of particular use is discovering the child's learning style.

It is unlikely that the child's dyslexia will be identified at the pre-school stage, since it is only when he begins his formal reading and writing work at nursery or school that the difficulties are shown up. The ways of working you decide on, together with the child and his carers, will depend on the child's age. Obviously, if the child is seven, he will need different books and materials from a child who is twelve or thirteen.

Whatever age the child is, he will usually have an **Individual Education Plan** (IEP) written for, and with, him. When you, as the primary practitioner (and maybe the learning support teacher or educational psychologist), plan an IEP, you should involve the carers and the child if possible. Your information can be pooled with the carers' knowledge to make sure that the IEP is effective. The IEP will include;

- which skills are going to be worked on;
- how they are going to be developed;
- who will be working with the child;
- how often the IEP will be used;
- how the child's success will be measured;
- when he should have achieved his targets;
- when the IEP will be reviewed.

When you choose the child's targets for the IEP, remember they should be **SMART**: Specific, Measurable, Achievable, Realistic, Time-scaled. For example, 'Fred will write the word bed three times correctly out of five attempts, for three successive mornings.'

It is important that you ask the carers to watch their child's progress in IEP activities he does at home and, if they have any worries, to consult you. The IEP can always be changed if it is not helping the child.

When you have all planned an IEP, the carers will probably be doing some activities with their child at home.

Here are some tips for **Happy Home-Sessions**.

- reassure the carers that if they are not sure how to do the activity, they may ask you to explain again or even demonstrate – it is important that they get it right;
- emphasise that if the child gets bored, distracted or distressed, he should stop doing the activity straight away. He can try again later;
- they should time the sessions well – not just before the child's favourite telly programme, or when he is starving and wants his dinner;
- if they think the activity is not helping the child to achieve his target, they should discuss this with you;
- they should stop when the child is on a winning streak, and always end the session by praising the child's efforts. You all want him to be keen to do the next session, so the carers should make home sessions fun and successful.

Case study

Rowena is eight years old and has been identified as having dyslexia. Her spelling is causing particular difficulty.

Rowena's parents and teacher have worked closely with the specialist teacher for dyslexia, to design an IEP aimed at developing Rowena's literacy skills.

Individual Education Plan

Child's name: *Rowena Smith*

DOB: *31.3.1999*

Date IEP implemented: *10.9.07*

Code of Practice level: *School Action Plus*

Areas of strength: *Knows five letter names & sounds (r,s,o,x,l) has some multi-sensory strategies for spelling; good with computer.*

Areas of difficulty: *Has difficulty with similar letters: b/d/p; f/t/k; m/n/u. Becomes distressed at every literacy session.*

Criteria for success:
1) Rowena will differentiate between 'b' and 'd' 4 times out of 5 in three successive sessions.
2) Rowena will differentiate between 'm' and 'n' 4 times out of 5 in three successive sessions.
3) Rowena will differentiate between 'f' and 't' 4 times out of 5 in three successive sessions.
4) Rowena will use the computer to prepare work for literacy sessions, using the 'buddy' system (Georgina to be buddy), reducing the number of episodes of distress by 3 per week.

Targets to be reached by: *8.12.07*

Teaching methods: *1:1 with Mrs Davies; 'buddy' Georgina; computer program 'Sounds & Looks OK'.*

Staff involved: *Mrs Davies, teacher; Mrs James, dyslexia specialist; Mrs Smith, mother, to work at home.*

Frequency of programme: *twice daily (morning and afternoon) for a maximum of ten minutes, five days per week; once per evening at home when possible*

Equipment/apparatus: *'Sounds & Looks OK' (Merrymaker Software); PC with sound card, coloured overlays; sandpaper letters; Plasticine.*

Date of next review: *8.12.07; to be attended by Mrs Davies, Mrs Smith & Mrs James*

How can I involve the child?

It is important that the child knows what is going on when you start to work with him and his carers. Even young children can be involved at a level that suits their understanding. Here are a few tips:

- speak to the child about his difficulties and why he needs support. Explain that you want to help him develop his skills because you love him;
- explain that you are all planning an IEP together to help him make progress. Being part of the team becomes very real and very important to him;
- make sure he understands the targets of his IEP.

If he sees what it is all about he will be happier at being involved and he will be keen;

- watch for any signs of stress and anxiety and talk calmly and positively to the child. Encourage him to share his fears with you;
- make sure the child is not scared about other professionals who become involved. Explain that these people have been specially trained to help children with the same type of difficulties as he has;
- allocate a key member of staff to the child. It is important for him to know there is one adult he can go to whenever he needs support, comfort or reassurance.

How is the child taught?

Our children are mostly taught through the senses of sight (visual) and hearing (auditory or aural), but a child with dyslexia may have difficulties with either or both senses.

Because of this, he may need to be taught using another sense, that of touch and movement (kinesthetic), giving the child an added 'tool' to use. This can involve many different ways of utilising the child's sense of touch.

Some examples include:

- using letters made out of sandpaper so the child can trace the letter-shape and actually feel it, as well as see it;
- encouraging the child to draw giant letters on the carpet, using finger and arms, so involving his whole body in the process;
- making the letters out of Plasticine or playdough, feeling the shape as he does so;
- writing giant letters in the air, 'feeling' the shapes as he makes them;
- using picture clues for particularly difficult-to-remember letters such as all the 'stick and ball' letters (p, b, d); for example,

Another commonly-used method of teaching a child with dyslexia is **VAKT** (Visual – Auditory – Kinesthetic – Tactile). Here, the word the child has to learn and remember is written on a card, using wax crayon, so the word has a texture the child can feel. Then the tutor will model the routine for the child, who then copies, as follows:

- say the word while simultaneously tracing it, then say it again;
- write the word, without looking at the card, then compare what the child wrote with the word on the card;
- repeat the first step until the child writes the word correctly three times without looking at the card for help.

Throughout all this, the child is allowed to draw pictures or use pictures or photographs that help him to remember the shape of the word, in much the same way as the example of 'bed' (*below left*)

Whatever method you as a team decide on for supporting the child, it is crucial to ensure that it is enjoyable for him, is achievable, and is meaningful.

Success and his self-esteem are the important factors here.

Pause for thought

What factors do you need to take into account when planning individualised work for a child with dyslexia?

Are there issues other than the child's basic performance or lack of progress which need to be addressed? What might these be?

If you are using a holistic approach, what aspects would have a bearing on how and what you plan together for the child? Make a list of things you think are relevant. Ask a colleague to do the same and then share your thoughts. Did you come up with a comprehensive list of considerations?

How can the setting support the child's carers?

One of the first and most important things you and the child's carers can do for the child is to help him to develop high self-esteem.

This means having a good picture of himself in his mind, which is crucial for successfully tackling difficulties he faces in life. Work closely with the child's carers to develop strategies for boosting his self-confidence, and so building a positive self-esteem.

What is self-esteem?

The picture we have of ourselves – our self-esteem – depends on how we think other people see us.

Two important factors decide how high or low our self-esteem is;

First is the type of person we are. If we are able to laugh off rude comments made to us, we can still have a good image of ourselves, ie., high self-esteem.

If on the other hand, we take unkind remarks to heart, and believe they are true, we can come to see ourselves as not worth very much, ie., have low self-esteem.

The second deciding factor is the importance we place on the people around us in our daily lives. For a child, the most influential people outside the family are likely to be the other children he mixes with, his peer group.

If the child is liked by the peer group for who he is, and not for what he can do, he is much more likely to have high self-esteem. Having caring friends is vital for a child to develop high self-esteem.

How can I help the child develop high self-esteem?

- Look at the way you behave towards the child in the setting. Try to think about the language you use and the attitudes you show. For example, do you say things like 'You should know that - you're a big boy now'? When a child is aware he has problems with his reading and writing, he can feel inadequate. If you think you say these things, often without realising, try to stop.
- Find ways to praise the child, particularly if he has made a real effort to do something, even if he fails. Let him know you are pleased when he tries hard. Tell him it does not matter if he has not yet managed to develop the skill he is aiming for, because you can see he is really having a go at getting it right.

- Be truthful when you praise the child. Do not tell him he is good at something unless he really is. He knows whether it is the truth, and false praise will not help him to develop confidence, neither will it help his self-esteem.
- Set him a target he can achieve without over-stretching him. This will give him some success, which in turn gives him the confidence to have a go again, or even have a go at something a bit harder.
- Help the child to practise skills he is aiming to develop. Practice is important to reinforce the target skill, so encourage him to do fun things that have practice and repetition built in.

What can I do in general to help the child if he has dyslexia?

You must help the child to face his problems. He is probably aware of his difficulties and he needs support in accepting this.

- Talk to him about his condition. He may feel that he is different from other children, but so is everybody, one way or another. Explain this to him. He needs to accept this difference and also to believe that there is help for him.
- Give him time and attention when he wants to talk to you. Listen to him sympathetically and tell him

you will do everything you can to help him.
- Find opportunities for the child to meet others who have difficulties or find something hard to do – let him know what it is you find very difficult to achieve. This helps him to realise he is not on his own.

With the child's carers, work out a programme of activities for the child to do at home.

Offer the carers these tips for **Happy Home-Sessions.**

Ask them to:

- give their child help and support with his home activity, but not to do it for him, especially if it is writing, spelling or maths work;
- follow work programmes in short bursts of activity to prevent the child from becoming tired and irritable;
- make sure the activities are fun to do and that their child continues to enjoy them;
- check for built-in progress in the programme so the child can see his hard work is paying off;
- give him games and activities specifically geared to his target skill – you (or the specialist professional) can advise about these;
- keep the routine consistent – this is crucial; if the child knows exactly what is going to happen during a session, he can concentrate on what he is doing without worrying about what comes next; get the carer to explain the game or activity before he starts;

- give the child time to practise new skills; he needs to feel confident in what he has learned before he moves on to the next target;
- let the child show off his new abilities to the rest of the family;
- encourage the child to develop the skills he is good at, such as sport, art or creative talents; let him join clubs or societies to help him in this.

How else can I support the carers to help the child?

Here are a few more tips for supporting the carers, and therefore the child.

- Work closely with the child's carers and pool your knowledge with them. This will help you to work out the best support programme. It is also important that the child sees you working together with his carers. This teamwork approach helps him to feel supported and cared for.
- Ask the carers to give you copies of any writing and spelling that the child does at home, so you can compare work in the setting with work at home. This will help to build up a picture of the errors the child is making, so ensuring that the plan of action is specifically targeted at the problems. More importantly and positively, it will build up a picture of the skills the child has already learned, and how you can help him to move forward with confidence from the point where he is now
- Help the carers to learn the strategies the child has learned for tackling difficult words or spelling rules. This will enable them to help him with his work, as well as helping him to practise and reinforce the techniques he has been taught.

Over the years many alternative and complementary 'remedies' have been put forward for helping children with dyslexia. We will look at some here, but it is important to remember that there is no quick fix or cure, and these suggestions may not work for the child you have concerns about.

Computers

The child should be familiar with using computers, which are in every setting, and are part of the teaching and learning process. Word processing

software can help the child in many ways for example with the following:

- checking spellings and giving practice through reading instructions;
- immediate reinforcement;
- essential over-learning;
- programmes with speech, making learning truly multi-sensory;
- learning to use databases and spreadsheets may aid sequential thinking and problem-solving skills;
- printouts are often easier to read than the child's own writing;
- allowing students to make and self-correct mistakes in private;
- ability to motivate students, being a truly multi-sensory, novel and stimulating way to learn. *

* From *Practical Strategies for Living with Dyslexia* by Maria Chivers (Jessica Kingsley Publishers, 2001)

You can find out about companies offering specialist software aimed at people with learning difficulties. See the contact details for Iansyst at the end of this book, and discuss with the child's carers whether he would be interested. Find out what your local authority has on offer and, again, share this with the child's carers.

Diet

There is evidence that many children with dyslexia are short of the vitamins or minerals which are vital to the development and maintenance of the brain and the body.

Fatty acids, iron and zinc are important elements that may be missing from a child's diet, and some carers give their child a supplement to make up the shortage. Many of them report a vast improvement in their child's performance and behaviour.

If you think a supplement could help the child, suggest the carers ask their doctor's advice about what would be best. Also get them to have a look at the child's general diet and decide whether it contains enough fresh fruit and vegetables (five portions a day is the recommended quantity), and whether the child is drinking plenty of water. Don't forget those vital proteins from meat, fish, eggs, cheese and milk.

Glasses, lenses and overlay sheets

Some researchers say that as many as 80% of children with dyslexia also have eye problems. These may arise from the child's sensitivity to light, which affects his vision.

People with dyslexia often report that when they are reading they see:

- words jumping around;
- words that seem to be faded;
- words jumbled up;
- letters in the wrong order;
- letters moving around;
- letters blending together;
- letters that seem to be fuzzy.

Tinted spectacles work very well for some children with dyslexia, and there are other things that help too. For example, some people have lenses similar to contact lenses, but with a minute speck of colour on them. These are called ChromaGen lenses and have helped many people with dyslexia to improve their reading ability and speed.

Then there is the Visual Tracking Magnifier (VTM) which is like a magnifying glass. It has a viewing strip in the centre about 1cm wide, with a patterned, transparent semicircle above and below it. The VTM helps to prevent distortion of the print as the child reads.

There are also transparent coloured overlays which can be placed on top of print, and the child reads the text through them. There are different colours and the child decides which one is comfortable for his vision.

Ask the carers to have their child's eyes tested either by a quality optician or through their doctor's recommendation to the eye clinic. Identifying an eye problem early on can save a lot of stress, difficulties and time later on.

Chiropractic

Chiropractic is an alternative therapy where the chiropractor works on the skull, the spine and the pelvis to correct any misalignment or dysfunction. It is thought that dysfunction like this affects the nervous system, and therefore has a bearing on dyslexia.

Many people with dyslexia feel that their reading ability is improved after a course with a chiropractor. If you think the child's carers would like to try it for their child, suggest they ask their doctor to recommend a reputable and qualified practitioner.

They need to be aware, however, that a course of chiropractic, which is rarely available on the NHS, can be quite expensive.

ARROW technique for hearing and listening

ARROW stands for *Aural – Respond – Read – Oral – Write*. It works by using recordings of the child's own voice. The recording is made when the child listens through a headset to the adult reading and then repeats it, reading the text himself at the same time.

After he has written the text, he checks whether it is correct. The programme of work is tied in with the National Curriculum, so the child's IEP can be planned around it. The ARROW method greatly helps the child's listening skills and so improves his reading and writing abilities too. Research is constantly being done into the effectiveness of different methods and systems.

Before you decide on one for the child, make sure you get as much information as possible about the reliability and professionalism of the organisations or people promoting them. Your setting's SENCO and LA specialist professionals will be able to help you and the child's carers in deciding the best approach for the child.

Other ways of offering the carers support

It is important that the child's carers feel confident in working with you. Some carers may have additional needs themselves, so you should take this into account, and make arrangements to ensure they are involved.

For example, if they also have dyslexia or they use alternative communication, you should approach this sensitively and make sure the carers are completely comfortable in their dealings with you. Ask them to let you know if they don't feel supported.

Problems caused by dyslexia are classed as special educational needs, and so the child and his carers have the right to any support and help offered by the LA. You or the SENCO must make sure you give the contact details of the local Parent Partnership Service (PPS) to the child's carers. This is an independent service set up to give parents and carers all the help and advice they want.

If English is not the carers' first language and they would like some support from somebody within their community with translation and even moral support, they have the right to ask for this. Check whether this is the case, and if so, you will need to get organised. If you arrange for an interpreter, make sure he is good.

Sometimes misunderstandings can happen because of a poor translation. Find out from your LA what provision, if any, is made through the department that deals with English as an Additional Language. Clearly there are cost implications involved in providing translation services, so you need to establish your setting's position in this regard. You also need to be careful that the language used during discussions is jargon-free, and carer-friendly, without being patronising.

Case study

Lewis' mother, Alison, attended a review to discuss his IEP, on which he had been working for three months. As well as dyslexia, he had speech problems, and was receiving support from the Speech and Language therapist (SLT). Alison had learning difficulties herself, and was unable to read.

During the review, the SLT described Lewis as 'intelligible', but went on to be fairly pessimistic about his progress, as were most of the professionals present. When Alison was asked for her opinion, she expressed how delighted she was that Lewis was doing so well. It transpired that she had misinterpreted 'intelligible' as 'intelligent'. This

example serves to warn professionals to be careful about the language they use during meetings.

If the child's carers have disabilities or difficulties and they would like help in working with you, let them know they need not be afraid to ask. There is plenty of support out there for them to use. Remember, they may have had a bad personal experience of special needs education, and so may be feeling uneasy. Hopefully times have changed and settings are much more sensitive and supportive than they used to be. It is important that you understand and keep this in mind when you're planning the child's programme together.

What if things go wrong between the setting and the child's carers?

The child and his carers have rights regarding the child's education, and your setting has a responsibility to make sure the child receives the support he needs to help him make progress.

If the carers have a disagreement with the way you are working with their child, try to sort it out directly with them first. Here are a few tips for dealing with the situation:

- keep calm and polite; try not to lose your temper, even if the carers are angry. A slanging match achieves nothing constructive for the child;
- arrange your meetings with the carers away from the children in the setting so you can talk together peacefully;
- make sure you stick to talking about the child; try not to be distracted by other things that have annoyed you, such as things said in temper which weren't relevant to the discussion;

what you are already doing, since they clearly feel unhappy with that. For example, 'Is there anything more, or anything different you could suggest I try with Fred to help?' or 'Do you know of anything else you would like me to do with Fred here in the setting?';

- follow up the meeting with a note confirming what was said. You could write something like, 'Thank you for seeing me yesterday. As we discussed...' Date the note and keep a copy;
- if they are still not happy, suggest you have another meeting, this time with the head or manager present as well. Again, keep calm and focused on the problem you are trying to solve. Follow up the meeting with a dated letter, giving an outline of what was agreed.

If the problem is still not resolved to the carers' satisfaction, let them know that they can go to the Parent Partnership Services (PPS) or the Independent Parental Support (IPS), which, though it is part of the LA, is totally impartial and is there to represent the parents' and child's interests. (Often the PPS is contracted out to a private source, to ensure freedom of bias.) The PPS is there to make sure that any problems between carers and settings or schools are sorted out fairly and amicably. Give them the contact details and reassure them that you are actually on their side, and wanting to resolve the problem for the child's sake.

From this chapter's contents, we can see how important it is for the child's progress to work in a positive, collaborative relationship with his carers. As long as you are all singing from the same song sheet, the child will be able to develop higher self-esteem, make progress and achieve the targets which you have all decided together he should aim for.

Pause for thought

Imagine you are working with a child who has dyslexia, and you are doing your best and more to support the child. If the child's mother approached you and accused you of doing nothing constructive to help her child, how would you react?

What would you do to defuse the situation? What would you offer the mother by way of sorting out the problem? Would you know where to go for support for yourself? Would you know how to ensure the mother gets a fair hearing of her grievances? How would you handle the situation regarding the child? Discuss this with a colleague.

How does the setting work with other professionals?

This section looks at the whole network of people who are involved with the child and who will be supporting him. Included in the team are, of course, the child's carers. They are the experts in their child and, as such, are to be considered as much a professional as anybody else.

First of all think about whether they need help. Assuming your relationship with them is positive and mutually understanding, you could try suggesting they look at their own situation with a fresh eye and decide if there is anything with which they would like some support. They might be dealing with other problems such as their personal relationships, other children in the family, general day-to-day routines or their jobs. If, on top of these problems, they are dealing with a child who has dyslexia, they may be totally overwhelmed. They could be feeling powerless to help their child and wondering where they can start. If they do have other problems, let them know they can get help and advice. Get them to think about where support could come from:

- their partner or spouse;
- their parents or parents-in-law;
- a brother or sister;
- a close friend.

Family or friends can help in a variety of ways. For example;

- they could occasionally baby-sit to give the carers some time to themselves, or a chance for them to have an evening out together;
- they could take the children out for a treat or a trip to give the carers some time in the house to do those things that they keep meaning to do and never get round to;
- they could have the child with dyslexia for an occasional 'sleepover' to give the carers and their other children some time together. (Brothers and sisters can feel left out and even jealous of the attention carers have to give to the child who has dyslexia.);
- they may have contacts, either personal or professional, who could give the carers some advice or point them in the right direction for more help;
- they could go with the carers to appointments with professionals to give a bit of moral support and also as an extra pair of ears in case the carers miss something important that is said.

Suggest to the carers that they could do some of the following:

- find out whether there's a local dyslexia support or self-help group and join it. They will meet other parents with the same problems who will give them advice, help and support. If there is not a local group, what about them starting one?;
- read books, leaflets or pamphlets about dyslexia; ask in the local library or the child's specialist support teacher where they can find the literature. Look on the internet and find information from the websites there;
- they should not become disheartened if they don't get the help they want for their child straight away – they should just keep trying and talk to as many people as they can about the problem.

What is your position in all this? It depends very much on your LA as to which other professionals you might work with in supporting a child with dyslexia. The age of the child will also be a deciding factor, as will the family's situation regarding the involvement of other professionals such as the health visitor or a social worker. On a day-to-day basis you will, of course, be working with your colleagues in the setting, who will be involved in helping to plan the child's programmes.

Let's take a closer look at some of the other professionals with whom you may be involved. Remember, it depends on your LA's practices which of these may become involved.

Learning support teacher

He is usually part of a team of specialised teachers employed by the LA. There is often one team for pre-school children and another for children of school age. He sometimes works closely with the educational psychologist.

Specialist dyslexia teacher

Your LA may have a teacher (or even a team) who specialises in working with children who have dyslexia. The specialist will test the child's learning skills in order to identify the severity of the difficulty. He may see the child in a centre where he is based or he may come into the setting; this depends on the system within your LA. How often he will see the child after the first meeting or two will depend on several factors. For example, how severe the dyslexia is, the plan of action to help and support the child, or what the workload of the specialist teacher is. The carers will almost certainly be invited to be involved in the plan of action by doing follow-up activities and games at home. They may be able to borrow some of the equipment that the specialist teacher uses in his sessions with the child.

Social worker

A social worker can offer support with many of the difficulties the carers face in their daily lives. You may need to reassure the carers that they should not be afraid that a social worker's involvement means they are going to have their child taken from them. A social worker's job is to help families, not to separate them (unless there is very good cause). A social worker can offer the carers advice, and also point them in the direction of other services or organisations. He will not necessarily become actively involved with the family, unless the carers ask for this, or if the family's difficulties are very worrying, but he will offer advice. You can put the carers in touch with the social workers' department, but if they prefer to make contact themselves, they will find the number under Social services in the 'phone book. They might speak to the duty social worker in the first place, but their local social worker will eventually get in touch.

Health visitor

The health visitor will give support if there are other children in the family who are young. You may or may not be directly involved with him. Again, this depends on how the system works in your area.

Educational Welfare Officer (EWO)

You may discuss with the carers whether it would help if the EWO were to become involved. He is attached to the education department of your LA and usually has social work training. His job is to work with children, parents and settings or schools to find the best solution to problems which are affecting the child. Some children with dyslexia develop emotional and behavioural problems which affect their schoolwork, and the EWO may be able to help.

Smile and the world Smiles with you.

Educational Psychologist (EP)

It is possible that you may become involved with an EP if he is the first point of referral in your authority. Every LA has EPs attached to it, and their job is to work with a child, his family and his teachers to tackle his problems. The EP can check what achievement level the child has, and then make good practical suggestions for ways that you and the carers can work together to help the child.

Family doctor

You could suggest that the carers also speak to their doctor (GP or General Practitioner) about the child's dyslexia. He is always there to give advice and support, and he also knows about many other services that are available. If he thinks one of those would be right for the child, he can put the carers in touch. The doctor might refer them to:

- the local health visitor;
- a counsellor;
- the child mental health service;
- the adult mental health service;
- the social services.

Child psychotherapist or child psychiatrist

If the child also has extreme behavioural or emotional problems, he may be referred to a child psychotherapist or child psychiatrist. The psychotherapist will discuss the child's problems with the carers, check the child's achievement level and then plan with the carers, and possibly with you, a programme of action. This can include many ways of helping. For example:

- family therapy;
- music therapy;
- play therapy;
- art therapy;
- counselling;
- behaviour therapy;
- psychological support.

There are also many voluntary organisations and societies that the child's carers can approach for help, for example, Dyslexia Action or Contact a Family. There may be a local family support group in your area. It is worthwhile suggesting the carers contact these organisations to ask whether they can help. If they do contact a voluntary organisation which offers to help, advise the carers to make sure they are qualified to offer support before they agree to become involved. Your social services office or your local library will have information about what is on offer in your area.

If the carers have access to a computer they can look on the internet. They can find local groups by typing the name of your area into the search window. For example, Parent support groups Dyslexia Leeds UK. This will bring up contact details of organisations which are in your area.

Your local authority should have a Parent Partnership Service which is there to give carers support. (In some areas it will be called the Independent Parent Partnership Service.) Whether your setting is state-maintained or a private establishment, if the carers are working with you to support their child with dyslexia, they can get in touch with this service.

Useful Contacts

The British Dyslexia Association
98 London Road, Reading, RG1 5AU
Tel: 0118 966 2677   Fax: 0118 935 1927
Email: helpline@bdadyslexia.org.uk   Website: www.bdadyslexia.org.uk

British Institute of Learning Disabilities
Campion House, Green Street, Kidderminster, Worcestershire, DY10 1JL
Tel: 01562 723010   Fax: 01562 723029
Email: enquiries@bild.org.uk   www.bild.org.uk

The Children's Legal Centre
University of Essex, Wivenhoe Park, Colchester, Essex, CO4 3SQ
Tel: 01206 872 466   Fax: 01206 874 026
Education Law Advice Line: 0845 456 6811
Email: clc@essex.ac.uk   www.childrenslegalcentre.com

Contact a Family
209 – 211 City Road, London, EC1V 1JN
Tel: 020 7608 8700   Fax: 020 7608 8701
Free Helpline: 0808 808 3555
Email: info@cafamily.org.uk   www.cafamily.org.uk

Dyslexia Action (formerly the Dyslexia Institute)
Park House, Wick Road, Egham, Surrey, TW20 0HH
Tel: 01784 222300   Fax: 01784 222333
Email: info@dyslexiaaction.org.uk   Website: http://www.dyslexiaaction.org.uk/

iansyst Ltd.
Fen House, Fen Road, Cambridge, CB4 1UN
Tel: 01223 420101
Email: reception@iansyst.co.uk ‘ Website: www.iansyst.co.uk
(This is a company that specialises in supplying computers and IT software to people with dyslexia.)

Network 81
1 – 7 Woodfield Terrace, Stansted, Essex, CM24 8AJ
Helpline: 0870 770 3306   Admin.: 0870 770 3262   Fax: 0870 770 3263
Email: info@network81.org   www.network81.org
(This is a national network of carers working towards properly resourced inclusive education for children with special needs.)

All these websites were accessed and contact details checked in October 2007.